Onwards
and
Upwards

Haydn Davies

British Library Cataloguing in Publication Data.

A catalogue record for this book is available from the British Library.

ISBN 978 0 86071 915 1

Published on behalf of the Author by

MOORLEYS
Print, Design & Publishing
info@moorleys.co.uk · www.moorleys.co.uk

The year was 2021 and Haydn's 70th birthday had come and gone in the summer. He wondered if it was time to record part, if not the whole of his story. Here then is only part of that story.

Onwards and Upwards

Haydn Davies

Haydn grew up in a happy home, had three brothers and a sister and all were cared for by Christian parents. The house was on a council estate designed and built after World War II and was very well planned and laid out with many green open spaces.

Technically the house was end of terrace. But that end was next to a large open field - once an early Briton fort. Many a happy hour was spent playing in that field with other children from 'the road' or 'the estate' and on bonfire night there were several bonfires on that field.

Mid 1960s

Haydn's parents were never too busy to spend time with any of them. They had a ministry that was based around the home. They led him to Jesus Christ.

It was this Jesus that was crucified as a perfect being for the sins of others, dead and was buried. After three days he was raised from the dead and offers this new life to all who will follow him.

At not quite five years old Haydn heard Jesus say, 'Follow me.' And he followed.

Nine years later he went through the waters of baptism. Then and there he declared publicly before friends and family that he would continue to follow his beloved master.

Haydn with dad outside the front door

Winter of 1963 – Haydn with his youngest brother, out the back door

A new teenager (13) in school uniform 1964

Haydn's sister, ten years younger, has Downs Syndrome. They faced questions of faith as a family and, as a ten-year-old, his parents helped him to accept the situation. In one sense the experience was his parents' experience – Ruth was their daughter and their responsibility. Ruth, they were told, would not live past twenty-one, but in the same year that Haydn was 70, Ruth was 60. Their parents had been promoted to glory in 1997 and 2000, but Ruth was still loved by her four brothers, but that is another story. *So, Haydn had a good grounding in the Christian Faith.*

Another home has been with Moira. They made home together wherever they lived. In the house in mid-Wales, they had their home and ministry. In the first weeks of ministry, they had to visit three families. Each family had suffered a tragic loss. Baptist College had not prepared him for those encounters.

But a faith in Christ that had been born in a Christian home and put to test in a great fire of experiences stood him in good stead. The life he'd shared with Moira also helped to hold him steady.

In between those two homes – the one with his parents and the home with Moira – he had another which was based around Cliff College in Derbyshire and it is there that this part of the story comes into focus. For it was there that he reached heights of joy and depths of sorrow. It was that period that his faith was more firmly tested and based. He reached cloud nine and rock bottom. Having reached rock bottom, he discovered who the Rock really was.

The college was indeed home.

At 20 years of age. Haydn learned of this College, which is primarily a Methodist College, but they took a reasonable percentage of other Christian denominations. In the early 1970s it was more of a Bible College with an emphasis on Evangelism. The course was basically a one-year course – with an option of doing a second if needed – and normally followed the academic year. They took a mere handful - 'a select few' – in January. Haydn learned of Cliff in the September (1971) and applied to start the following January (1972). He was asked why he did not want to wait until the following September. His answer was that he had applied to the Christian Colportage Association (CCA) to do door to door evangelism. The CCA asked him to reapply when he was 21 (in June 72). So, he wanted to make the most of his time in getting some training. Cliff College accepted him and so early in January he left home for the first time.

Official College Year Photograph of College Year 71-72

It was Saturday 8 January. There were eight who started that day. The weather was heavy snow. His mam and dad were quick in making sure he was safe before attempting their journey home. Having unpacked he made his way to the common room. Being the first there he started to read the paper that had been left for the students benefit. It wasn't

6

long before another student walked in. 'Hello', she said, 'I am Rosemary. Who are you?"

Haydn always had a speech problem. Even in the local village shop in mid Wales, where he had served for a while, he was known as Arkwright! For years his parents had tried to sort the problem. So, when this beautiful young lady asks his name, he is tongue tied, he stammers. So, she helped with the problem. Haydn did only the one year and left at the end of that calendar year. It was home to him as well as college.

In the September – the start of his last term he started having blackouts. This was later - 1982 - diagnosed as an uncommon form of epilepsy. All of these attacks were brought on by emotional strain. They started in college, when there were the prospects of new relationships. He was aware of one in particular. Haydn had noticed, for instance, that Rosemary had gone the extra mile for his 21st in the June and he longed to respond but even then, he struggled. The doctor later said in 1983 that it was a rare form of epilepsy. These blackouts would continue until February 2012.

Also in that September, he did the first 'Clinic Service' of the new academic year as one of the students who had already spent time in the college. One of his hymns was "This, This is the God we Adore" by Joseph Hart (some books have it as 'How Good is the God we Adore'). The second verse reads: "It is Jesus the first and the last whose Spirit will guide us safe home; *we will praise Him for all that is past and trust Him for all that's to come.*" How those words have taken on a deeper meaning.

In December the college had the Christmas Dinner. Students and staff dressed up – suits and ties for all male students - and tables were laid for the special occasion. Each student had a reserved place with a name plate marking where they should sit. On that name plate was a Scripture. Haydn's read: "Thou crownest the year with thy goodness. Psalm 65.11." It was an emotional evening. He was saying farewell to the college – a true home for him. A home where, despite the blackouts, he had been truly happy and he could really say "Thou crownest the year with thy goodness."

The 12 months then that he spent at the College were very formative. It was there he made friends that would stand the test of time. Haydn was later, in 1996, asked to join the CC Fellowship committee – this looked after matters of the alumni. He served on that committee as minute secretary, Chair, and pastoral secretary. The motto of the college is still *"Christ for all and all for Christ!"* That is, preach and offer Christ to all - and give all you have and are to Christ! So, he learned more about himself during his time at the College and he continued to give it all back to Christ whom he was also getting to know better.

At 21½ Haydn left the college - at the end of 1972 - and joined the CCA early in 1973 and was based in Sheffield.

Christmas 1973 Haydn spent at home in south Wales but he had to be back in Sheffield between Christmas and New Year. So, he agreed with a friend that on New Year's Day, sometime during the day, he would commit the coming year to God by using the words of the Irish Hymn '**Be Thou My Vision O Lord of my Heart.**' The last verse has these words, or similar, depending on which hymn book you use:

> '**High King of heaven, after victory is won,**
> **Still be my heaven's joy thou bright heaven's sun.**
> **Heart of my own heart whatever befall,**
> **Still be by vision, thou Ruler of all.**'
> **(Translated: Mary Elizabeth Byrne)**

Note those words **"Whatever befall."** So New Year's Day Haydn caught the bus from Sheffield to Bakewell and walked the 15 miles back. At a quiet point he sang those words. If he had known then what would happen, would he have meant those words?

So, this period came to an end in 1974. Haydn had a big trauma that gave him a massive blackout - one that lasted three whole days blacked out. This one blackout remains the quickest and longest blackout that Haydn ever had. All the others took at least 30 minutes to come on but this one was almost instantaneous. All the others lasted two hours at most – this one lasted three days It was at that moment that *he felt that pain of searing loss:* this has stayed on Haydn's memory until this day. He still had tears and nightmares until the early 2000s.The doctor recommended that he return home – back to Newport. Job chapter 1 verse 21 comes to mind at this point.

There is a hymn with the first line: **"How firm a foundation ye saints of the Lord, is laid for your faith in his excellent word…"**

Two verses stand out.

"When through the deep waters I call you to go,
The rivers of grief will not you overflow.
But I will be with you in trouble to bless
And sanctify to you your deepest distress.

"The soul that on Jesus has leaned for repose,
He will not, He cannot desert to its foes.
That soul, though all hell should endeavour to shake,
He will never, no, never, no never forsake."
('K' in Rippon's Selection)

So, at 23, having been away from home for three years, he returned back to Newport, his family, and his work with the council. He had kept three things from that period: his blackouts, his memories, and his faith in the Lord Jesus. In his early years he had the pain of bronchitis. This had passed only a few years earlier but now had become the pain of these blackouts which reached their worst in 1980 when, in the last six months of that year, he averaged two a day. But in 1974 he had already reached rock bottom and he found that the rock was Jesus Christ. That was to be his continued strength until his dying day! His work with the council continued until 1987. He also renewed his membership at Nant Coch Church. There he stayed until the early 1980s when he became a Baptist. More of that later.

The blackouts were brought on by emotional strain. They started in college when relationships were new and under constraint. They certainly intensified after the trauma. Every time Haydn tried to put the story into words the blackouts would start. So it was that his parents saw these attacks but did not know the reasons for them.

The doctors had in those days given him some strong tablets which were strictly regulated. They did help to lessen the blackouts but within three months of the trauma he almost took an overdose. It was two good friends that realised what was happening and at the very last minute flushed those tablets down the loo. So, the doctors refused any more medication for a long time.

To add pain to pain that was already heart breaking there were those well-intentioned but misguided people who gave their counsel: "Haydn had done some wrong so God has punished him." And as the days turned into weeks some would ask, "Where is your faith? Surely you must be lacking in faith."

Friends such as the two just mentioned and his minister at the time were a great help. Haydn remembers being taken to the Manse where he was allowed to sob his heart out. The minister showed no embarrassment but simply allowed Haydn that space and time that he needed.

The doctor at that time advised him to return to South Wales and as he heeded that advice it seemed as if the whole period – 1972-1974 – had ended in failure. It seemed that Haydn had nothing to show for those three years.

Rosemary and Haydn had exchanged book marks. His to her read: *"God is love. All the paths he leads you on, even the darkest one will end in glory. Keep your eyes fixed on this goal and your heart will be strengthened and immersed in joy."* Hers to him reads: *"Those who suffer are the first to find their way to God's heart. A child in tears belongs in the father's arms."*

Through all of this Haydn never lost his faith. He had always believed that Jesus Christ died and was raised from the dead for him. He still believes that He gives this life to those who trust in Him. Because of that Haydn has learned how to handle that experience so that he can share with other people in such a way that they too reflect on their own faith in similar circumstances. We are ministers of Him who shows us his hands and side and says, **'Peace be with you.'**

How much was God the Father's heart broken when Jesus died upon the Cross? What went on in Heaven when Jesus suffered for you and me? Haydn knew what was in his heart when the trauma struck. He felt the pain in the Father's heart was incomprehensibly greater. Those wound prints in Jesus' hands are a constant reminder what the Godhead went through for our salvation.

It was shortly after this that Haydn wrote these words:

[1] The Father was silent the day Jesus died; The Father was silent the day that he cried And Heaven was silent when he bore my sin; No help from above was offered to him.	[3] He hung there and suffered, and he died alone. He died there in anguish my sins to atone. He bore all my sin so I could go free: This help from above was offered to me.
[2] He cried, "You forsake me! O my God, why?" 'My God, you forsake me!' was his anguished cry: But Heaven stayed silent, there was no reply, And Jesus was left on the Cross to die.	[4] But death could not hold him, he rose from the dead. The grave could not keep him, he's our living head. He rose all victorious his foes to remove; And yes, we can know his help from above.

So, by the end of that summer Haydn returned to the family home in South Wales. There he was surrounded by family and friends. He took up his membership in his home church and went back to his work for the local council. And there he stayed: working, worshipping, and still grieving. How he longed to be able to tell someone his story in more depth. But the more he tried, the worse were his blackouts. These blackouts lasted until 2012 – the last one being in the early February of that year.

The period 1974 to 1984 is the next part of the story. They say it is always darkest before the dawn and that describes that period in Haydn's life.

Having renewed his membership with his home church, Haydn attended all the regular activities – Sunday worship, both morning and evening, midweek prayer meetings and bible studies, and helped with the youth work. One Monday prayer meeting in 1978, a prayer was made that started Haydn in a new direction. Someone else in that prayer gathering prayed for those countries from which we never heard any news. He then prayed for countries by name, and the first on that list was Albania. Haydn remembers no other names on that list but remembers thinking, 'Where on earth is Albania?' He went home from that meeting, discovered where it was, and that, at the time, declared itself to be the world's first and only genuine atheistic country. He discovered that there was a prayer meeting for Albania in London. He started going to it regularly and in 1979 made his first visit to that land of darkness. It was a darkness that could be felt.

In 1980, Oak Hall, a Christian 'holiday' company had organised a camping tour across Bavaria and Czechoslovakia (now split into two countries – the Czech Republic and Slovakia) Haydn was on that trip. The group was to meet at Sheerness.

Haydn remembered very well the journey to Sheerness to meet the rest of the party. They had to be there by 11.00am on the Saturday in June. There was no way he could be there by leaving South Wales Saturday morning so Haydn had gone in to the local station to book a berth on the overnight train. When he spoke to the person at the booking office, he was told that there was no sleeper. Haydn was able to show a timetable that advertised it. The booking clerk immediately rang Swansea and after a short discussion it was agreed to put the sleeper on the train and so Haydn had a bed while travelling to Paddington. Thus, he was in London in comfortable time to get to Sheerness and to join the party. The evening before he left for that trip Haydn had gone for a quiet walk and had resolved before God that he would stay single for the rest of his life if that was God's will. Such was the grief that he still felt over the trauma of 1974.

So, the Oak Hall trip was to be 'an adventure' with others – but he would not look for friendship beyond that. Within a few days he had, however, met a young lady from Croydon. After that trip they met several times over the next three years: Haydn travelling often to Croydon, and she to South Wales. During that period several things happened. Haydn's blackouts increased. The last six months of 1980 he was averaging one a day. Some days he was clear other days he was having two or three. How on earth he managed to keep working in itself was a miracle. They did ease back in the following years and, as noted earlier, they finished completely. Towards the end of 1981 Haydn moved out of his parents' home into a flat in a nearby village and, as a consequence, he changed his church membership: he became a Baptist.

Two other things happened in 1981.

Haydn purchased in February 1981 a very old VW Beetle. The previous owner - still a good friend many years later - had driven it back and forth into Eastern Europe and so there was a high mileage on it. It was sold to him for £10 (ten pounds!) simply as a run about! That is locally!! Haydn lived then in Newport, South Wales. Other friends lived in the south of France (below Lyon) and they invited him down to stay for a week. Haydn was due to return to Albania in August 1981 and his friends had invited him down so they could spend time together

13

praying about the Albania trip. More about that later. So, Haydn went to the south of France and, yes, you guessed it, he went in that car. He left home on the 17th July and he made it there and enjoyed his stay.

On the way home - 25th July - Haydn drove through Paris, yes through Paris, and was on the road to Calais when the car came to a halt just short of Beauvais.

The nearby garage could not help - just a shrug of the shoulders. So, Haydn rang his friends in the south who gave him the phone number of the OM (Operation Mobilisation) mechanic in Paris.

The main mechanic came out with two helpers and took Haydn back to Paris. They gave him bad news - his engine was dead - and some good news. They had had another beetle towed in that day with a rotten body but a live engine. It was about the same age as the other one. That Saturday night Sunday morning they simply changed the engines. The two helpers started a discussion about working on the Sabbath and did the Sabbath start at 6.00pm on Saturday or at midnight.

The main mechanic pulled himself out from under the car and said, 'It does not matter: the donkey is in the ditch and needs pulling out.' Haydn is still not sure if he meant the car was the donkey or Haydn was the donkey!!? When the job was done and Haydn had the bill, he was simply charged for items new out of his stock room. He did not charge for the engine for he had not paid for it himself. So, Haydn arrived home over 24 hours late in the early hours of Monday 27th July - but in this car.

The reason Haydn had gone to the south of France was to stay with friends and spend some time preparing for a trip to Albania in that August. Albania was a closed communist country. Only certain people were allowed out; and to get in you either had to be a diplomat from a county recognised by the Albanian government, or a tourist with an Albturist tour.

Haydn had his booking with Albturist for the dates 10-22 August. As far as Albturist and the Albanian government were concerned he was a tourist along with the other members of the touring party (whom Haydn did not know!). But his week in France with his friends led them to believe that he should take in copies of *John's account of the Gospel* into Albania. The Albanian government had banned all religious literature from within its borders. Anyone found in possession of such faced life imprisonment, or death. Anyone trying to take it in ran the same risks.

On 10 August, Haydn joined the other tourists at Heathrow. The Albanian government allowed no private vehicles in Albania, nor could they fly into Albania, either directly or indirectly. The trip was a flight to Belgrade, then a coach to the Yugoslavian (as it was) border via Titograd. They then walked across no-man's land and checked in through their passport control and customs. That could take a while. Each 'tourist' was given a custom's form to fill in and one of the questions asked was: 'Are you carrying any literature?'

15

That could be a newspaper, paperback, or Albanian guide book – any literature meant any literature. They wanted to vet it. Haydn answered the question simply as yes.

In Albania 1981

Haydn can't remember how many were on that trip but they were several in number. There were only two custom officials on duty and they were working together examining each tourist's luggage. The one would take and read the form, while the other asked for cases to be opened.

Haydn was half way down the line and everyone in front of him had their cases thoroughly checked. Everyone behind him also had their cases checked thoroughly searched. He knew that if they opened his cases they would find ***John's account of the Gospel*** on top of his clothes, and not hidden. Haydn reached the 'desk', handed over his form, and was waved straight through. No attempt was made to open any of his luggage.

The rest of the group was as amazed as he was, but because he knew none of them, Haydn could not give any explanation as to what just happened. He knew that God had answered prayer in a real way and allowed him to take the Christian Gospel into this atheistic country.

Just one of many propaganda signs in Albania 1981
This one outside the hotel in which Haydn was staying

Albturist planned the dates of their trips with some thought. In having to pick one group up at the border, it was also dropping the previous tour off for their exit from Albania. Somewhere in transit there were two groups that could have contact with each other. On this exiting group were two Christians from Cardiff who knew Haydn well. They also had taken Christian literature into Albania and had been spotted trying to distribute it. Their passports had been stamped as not being welcomed again into the country. They were told that if they had been men, they would have faced imprisonment or death.

On their way out they spotted Haydn and made themselves scarce. They knew they were being watched by security. If they had been seen speaking to Haydn, then he too would have been watched. Ten days later, when he returned to South Wales, the three met up and shared experiences. They were a bit down hearted because of their experience. Yet they rejoiced that all of the literature had been left behind in Albania. Theirs with security officials who, they prayed, would read it; Haydn's with other Albanians whose names he may not know.

All this has encouraged him to share his faith publicly down through the years since, wherever he might be. It was the Lord Jesus who said, '*All* authority in heaven and earth has been given to me. Go therefore into *all* the world and preach the Gospel...'

It must be noted that these last two stories – the trip to France in the beetle, and the one to Albania with the literature – happened in 1981. While the worst of his blackouts were over at the end of 1980, they were still happening until 2012.

There was no medical insurance for Haydn's trip to Albania. Before he went his mother pleaded with him not to go. Because Haydn knew about his mother's faith, his answer remained the same: 'Better to be in Albania and in God's will, than to stay at home and out of God's will. That was the safest place to be.'

As for the trip to France, his doctor had advised caution. He left home on the Friday and it took him three days to get there, sleeping on the back seat if needed. Those at home were concerned. When Haydn did not appear from France as planned on the Saturday night, there was much worry in the home in south Wales. On the Sunday night – about 10.00 pm, when Haydn arrived in Folkstone, he found a public call box, and rang home. His fathered answered and Haydn assured him that he was alright, and would be home in the small hours of Monday, and that dad should go to bed. Haydn arrived home at about 3.00am

18

on the Monday and dad was still up waiting (and mother still awake!!) and worrying.

And on both these trips in 1981 there was the concern, love, and prayer of a new friend – the young lady from Croydon. Haydn had shared with her a little of what was happening, and what had happened. By the time he had left for France, the two of them had known each other for one whole year and been several times seeing each other on weekends. She had been told about the trauma in 1974, and his return to South Wales, the blackouts, the trip to Albania in 1979. She had, over the 12 months, witnessed several of the blackouts including the severe frequency of the latter part of 1980. So, when Haydn was planning the 1981 trips, as one of his newest friends, she was very concerned. But she became aware of the prayer, and the answers to those prayers the longer she was with him. Those two weeks away, especially the Albania trip, tested their new friendship.

It was at the end of 1981 that Haydn moved out of the family home to a nearby village. That caused him to change church and he became a Baptist. There had been two people involved in helping with those decisions. The one was the friend from Croydon, of course. The other was his uncle Ifor. Ifor was his mother's brother, and had lived in New Zealand for many years. He had come back to Wales for a ten-week holiday in order to get his name on the Newport housing waiting list. Ifor gave Haydn a 'friendly' bet – which of the two could get a council flat first? Haydn won the bet. Before Ifor returned to New Zealand to work his retirement notice, Haydn had his new flat.

This flat was originally built for the more senior people of Newport and area. But because of its more remote location and shortage of public transport many of the flats remained unoccupied. It belonged to the *Wales and West Housing Association,* and it were they that contacted Newport to see if there were any youngsters needing accommodation. Haydn's opportunity was there and then and he moved from his parents' home to live on his own.

His Croydon friend was still concerned about Haydn's health. The move meant he was further from church and he had no car to get there. Public transport was zero on Sundays in those days. She suggested to Haydn that he look for another church nearer home, and so he became a Baptist. This helped his workload, for in his previous church, Haydn had been very involved with many things. What with normal work, and church life, there was no time 'to call his own.' Now for the time being, he was just a member of the congregation. This helped in reducing Haydn's blackouts quite considerably for which he was grateful for the advice and help given.

The period between 1980 – when they met, - and 1983 was a period when both of them were trying to understand God's plan for both of them. Were they meant to be together or not? In that instance it was decided that in 1983 they should go their sperate ways. She did not know if she could cope with those blackouts all the time. There did not seem to be either an answer to control them or an end to them. So, at the end of May 1983, they decided it was best to go their own ways. What happened then to his Croydon friend is another story that can only be told by her.

We noted above that Haydn had met Moira one cold February Sunday night in 1981. This was part of that period mentioned above - *the period 1974 to 1984 is the next part of the story. They say it is always darkest before the dawn and that describes that period in Haydn's life.*

Haydn was still seeing his Croydon friend at that point but he and Moira were members of the same church. So, when Haydn was no longer going to Croydon he began to settle into a new routine for a while: living in his flat, working for the council, getting involved in the new church he was attending. It was simply routine. The church had two buildings: the smaller one only had about thirty attendees but they were also part of the other fellowship at the other end of the village. Haydn attended the smaller one for most things but for the young people's group after church on Sundays he went to the other fellowship. Moira played the piano at the smaller fellowship. In the July of '83 the young people's group were going to hear a choir in yet another church after the main evening service, and Haydn said he would meet the rest of the group at that church. He attended the smaller church's evening service. As Haydn was about to leave for the choir, he asked Moira if she would like to go with him: she said yes. And so started a new chapter in his life. That was in the July 1983. Within thirteen months they were married. They were engaged in the October of '83 and married the following August.

11 August 1984

*With both set of parents, bridesmaids Ruth and Claire,
and Best Man Allan Parsons*

With bridesmaids Ruth and Claire, and Best Man Allan Parsons

At about the same time Haydn was feeling led to do something about being in the pastoral ministry. He had been asked as an eight-year-old what he would like to be when he grew up. His reply than was that he wanted to be a minister. Now in his early thirties Haydn began to do something about it. Moira agreed that they should look it seriously.

The Baptist way of exploring ministry was new to them so Haydn approached their minister who set things in motion. The superintendent was approached and he informed them that Haydn had to get the blessing of his own church first. This was done by taking a church service, including the preaching. Then the church should recommend, if deemed appropriate, to the local Baptist Association Ministerial Recognition Committee. At that point there should be three more services to be taken. If it was still favourable, the recommendation would then go to the Baptist College most appropriate. In Haydn's case this was the college in Cardiff.

The journey had begun and things seemed to going well. His own church, and the Association were happy to recommend him. But the college seemed to have other ideas. They had received a medical report from Haydn's doctor.

When Haydn had moved at the end of 1981, he had to change doctor's surgeries. The one where he had to register was in Rogerstone. Others who attended that surgery recommended that he keep away from a certain doctor, but Haydn was still having his blackouts and was in need of seeing a doctor again. An appointment was made. Haydn was glad that he kept that appointment. Whilst the doctor's 'bed side manner' was terrible he knew what the cause of Haydn's blackouts was. A rare form of epilepsy. The doctor prescribed medication that was so strong he was unable to drive for a little while. But it began to control the blackouts. But the doctor was asked for a health check for Haydn going into college. Could he cope with that pressure? And he was also newly married.

The college sent Haydn away and asked him to reapply again in a few years if he still felt it was the call of God. Would he never be free of the chains of these blackouts? At the end of 1986 Haydn and Moira talked it over again and felt it right to pursue the matter again.

The journey began again and things went well. His own church, and the Association were both happy to recommend him – again. Should Haydn reapply to the college in Cardiff or should he try another? Spurgeon's in London? Or Bristol?

For practical reasons – they had a home in Rogerstone, Newport, and Moira could carry on teaching – the college in Cardiff was approached again. This time Haydn was asked to have a medical from his doctor before he met the college senate. And this time the medical was more certain that he could cope with the four-year course. The blackouts were still there, but less frequent and less severe. The college then invited him to meet the senate for another interview.

One of the questions posed this time was: What had Haydn been doing between the two interviews, considering they were a few years apart?

There were two things.

The first was that his home church – Bethesda Rogerstone had asked him to join the diaconate. That gave him some experience as to how Baptist churches were run.

The second was that he had done a correspondence course with London Bible College. This was in New Testament Greek. This had been successfully completed. The collage senate accepted him to do a four-year course. Three in the Diploma in Theology (Dip TH) and one year on the Diploma in Pastoral Studies (DPS).

Haydn then started the course in the September of 1987. He had two gripes. Why did he need to do the fourth - pastoral studies – year? He was a mature student, and had enough skills in that area without having to spend another year 'learning' about it. Having done that year, 1990-91, Haydn was more convinced that, for him, it was a waste of time.

His second gripe? He was expected to do the New Testament Greek course while there in Baptist College. It meant starting from scratch again, when he had already mastered it with the London Bible College. Nevertheless, he did the full course. His marks in the Greek were very high. Haydn studied The Gospel according to Luke in the first year, 1 John in the second, and Romans in the third. On the day he sat his final Greek exam, the exam was due to last three hours, but after 90 minutes he raised his hand to indicate he had finished. Both in his first year and in the third Haydn won the NT Greek prize at the Baptist college end of year service.

During Haydn's final year – that DPS year – his name went on the Ministerial List as a student now looking for a pastorate. In the initial explorations Haydn said he was willing to go anywhere. So, his details were sent to various places.

During that final year Haydn was placed with Revd Gareth Evans at Richmond Road Baptist Church, Pontnewydd. Gareth's family background was from mid-Wales and in the first few weeks of Haydn's placement, Gareth had heard that there was a pastoral vacancy in Radnorshire. Would Haydn consider it? Haydn's first reaction was to turn 'his nose up' at the prospect. His name had been sent to other – much better? – places. But he did allow his name to go forward and it was sent to a group of four churches known to some as the Maesyrhelem group. The other three churches in that group were The Pound (or Hepzibah), The Gravel, and Penithon. At first his heart was not there: he, and Moira, were hoping for a less rural setting. Places like Maidstone, and Bournemouth, and churches in Leicestershire were all explored. But God's call was clear. For now, it was to be mid Wales.

The Manse in the deep winter of the early 2000s

Anyone starting in their first ministry within a Baptist Union church had to serve three years in that pastorate to be transferred to the full accredited list. There were other things as well to be done: books to read, and be involved in Association and Union events. So, when Haydn and Moira accepted the call to mid-Wales, his mother said they would not like it and would not last very long. Haydn's response was to say they would do those three years and then review the situation. Twenty-five years later they retired from there.

And what a quarter of a century it was. Years of tears and laughter; years of joy and of sorrow; years of satisfaction and frustration. Some of that story may not yet be told because it involves person or persons still living. It would be unfair on either them or their families to bring up the heart break and anger again. There had been Blessings of Children, Weddings, and Funerals; there had been work in the communities and in various schools; there had been various groups of children and youth work.

In the early years there were those who continued to come and play table tennis long after others had stopped coming to youth club and some came to the Manse once a month on a Sunday evening.

There was a Youth Club at the Pound, and Family Services in all four churches.

They also had sessions shared with the Church people on Friday nights at the New Inn. (It was said that they should change the style of services. Here they changed the venue and style.) Also, on Sunday nights at Maesyrhelem they had once a month something for the youngsters. This again was a different approach.

They had a Holiday Bible club where 16 youngsters from across the group and area came to Maesyrhelem. These youngsters had a good time and asked if there were more.

In Haydn's last three or four years they had, on a fortnightly basis, the JAM (Jesus and Me) club where over half of the local primary school came on a Wednesday late afternoon straight from school. There were six chapel members helping out and craft work, and games like table tennis were played. At least three of the *Friends and Heroes* series were shown sharing stories from both the Old and New Testaments.

Haydn had been into the High School in Llandrindod and taken assemblies. He admitted that this was not an experience he enjoyed but take Assemblies in High School he did.

When Haydn and Moira moved into Mid Wales, the chapels belonged to the Baptist Union of Wales (BUW), and the Radnorshire and Montgomeryshire Baptist Association (Rads & Monts Bap Ass). The chair (man) of the Association youth committee rang Haydn to ask if Haydn would become the secretary of that committee. The first question that was asked was, 'Who else is on that committee?' The answer was given and Haydn discovered that, if he joined, he would be, at forty, one of the youngest committee members. So, he took up the appointment and began to recruit younger members to serve as well. The voices of experience were kept and the committee began to do things.

The BMS World Mission had started a gap year for youngsters. These youngsters would spend about six months somewhere where the mission had personnel working: India, Nepal, Albania, Brazil, Italy, and France to name but a few. They would then return and tour the UK to share their experience and to inspire others. The BMS coordinator for Wales contacted Haydn to see if either he or the youth committee could organise something. The coordinator had done this role for a few years but wanted someone else to do it. Haydn took this on board with the committee's backing and support.

When this was fully developed, the Action Teams were in mid Wales for a fortnight. Sometimes it was one team for two weeks, or it was two teams doing a week each. This latter was sometimes the same week, but often it would be two separate weeks. The teams would visit the schools across the county (Powys) so this involved the Breconshire Baptist Association being involved as well. At the best, the teams would visit four High Schools, at least 15 Junior schools, four or five churches, and either one or two Baptist Associations over the two-week period. The logistics was a challenge. Powys is the biggest county in Wales, (possibly the UK?) and they needed to be in one part of the county each day. But the committee under Haydn's direction was able to have an effective programme. This included finding meals at lunch times. All the other meals were provided by the hosts. The committee in general, and Haydn in particular, was grateful to Dr David and Mrs Sue Wilson for hosting many of these teams.

There were weddings and funerals, dedication services for young children and their parents, and services of believer's baptism. After his retirement in 2016 Haydn was asked what was the youngest person he had ever baptised. His answer was a ten-year-old. On the same day he also baptised a twelve-year-old. They were two sisters, and their father was baptised the same day. As a Baptist, Haydn practised neither infant baptism (christening) nor adult baptism. It was Believer's Baptism that was practised and these two sisters, even at ten and twelve, acknowledged Jesus as their Lord and Saviour.

Haydn also served as President of the Rads and Monts Bap. Ass. He also went on to serve as the President of the BUW English speaking Assembly, twice!! Both occasions the term of office was one year vice president, one year president, and one year as the immediate past president. The first-time round, the annual meeting, when he was inducted, was held at Maesyrhelem, and members from across his pastorate helped with catering.

During that first term of office Haydn was privileged to also attend the Annual Meetings of the Welsh speaking Assembly of Wales, the Baptist Union of Scotland, and the Baptist Assembly in Blackpool. This last one was the Assembly of BUGB and BMS. He also attended the National gathering of Quakers and the Church in Wales general synod. The Free Church Council for Great Britain also had an annual dinner for the 'leaders' of the different denominations and Haydn received an invitation. This was held in Tavistock Square, London. As for the meal in Tavistock Square, the first course the guests were allowed to sit wherever, and with whomever they wished. When that course finished, the guests were asked to look for a number. There were only three numbers, 1,2,3. The numbers 1 were asked to stay where they were seated, the numbers 2 were asked to move to the table on the one side, while the numbers 3 went the other way. The same happened at the end of the main course. So, each course saw us talking with different guests from different denominations.

In the second term of presidency, he led a mission awareness trip to Nepal in 2018. They were a team of eight members from across south and mid Wales.

Megan – front row far left – is based in Nepal and was their 'guide'
The other eight from Wales

An evening meal together

Haydn in Nepal

Haydn's spirit was vexed in him at the many Idols in Nepal
There was also much poverty in the land
But the Christian workers are doing a great job in sharing the Gospel

In the year following the trip to Nepal - 2019 he and Moira had an invitation to a Buckingham Palace for a garden party.

Outside Buckingham Palace – 21 May 2019

In the very back garden after the party 21May 2019

Haydn had also kept his interest in Albania. The BMS World Mission had begun to place workers in that land. That was because in the early 1990s Albania had begun to open up. It got rid of the atheistic communists and began to adopt more freedom in religion and politics.

The Pastorate which Haydn and Moira were ministering in had been linked with Dr Suzanne Roberts as she served in both Bangladesh and Mozambique. She had returned to the UK to explore a call to Pastoral Ministry. Her first church was in Presteigne, a church which belonged to the Association where Haydn and Moira were placed. Because of this connection, while Suzzanne was on Probation (as it was called in those days!!) Haydn was asked to be her Senior Friend – these days called a Mentor.

This meant that the Pastorate was without a link through BMS to mission personnel. This was in 1996. The office in Didcot was contacted. Roger and Nikki Pearce had recently been accepted for service and were shortly going to serve in Albania. At that point in time, they had one child, a second child was born soon afterwards. Haydn visited Albania a few times in that period and saw the Pearces and they also visited mid Wales to share with the churches the news of what they were doing. It has been a joy and privilege to be linked with that family.

(In 2018, when Haydn led a Baptist Union of Wales team to Nepal, he and Julie Prince, his co leader, met with Roger in Didcot. Roger had changed roles and was now responsible for much of Asia for BMS and this included Nepal.)

During the early 1990s Haydn had begun to make friends with some Albanians. This came about because in 1992 he went looking for another couple who went to Albania with BMS.

On the way to the address in Tirana he had been given, Haydn, with a friend from England who could speak Albanian, stopped to ask for directions. The two who were asked did not tell them, but took them.

Then waited for them and walked back to the hotel with them. These two were introduced to the group's translator who was able to communicate better with them as to why we were in Albania. The Gospel was shared with them and they were put into contact with a local church. One of those two was Mirlinda, from Korce. There had been a church in Korce before the communists tried to extinguish it. Mission personnel started going to Korce and discovered three men who had 'kept the faith'. Others were now coming to faith, and they were encouraged to gather with the mission personnel, and those three warriors of faith, who had kept the light burning. Mirlinda joined that church in the early 1990s and is still an active member there.

Mirlinda and Haydn exchanged addresses and started to communicate with each other. There were no emails in the early '90s, nor FB, Messenger, or ZOOM. In those early days it was all done by snail air mail. Mirlinda's English was very minimal and Haydn's Albanian was even less.

When her letters arrived, he had to find someone to translate for him, and Mirlinda had to do the same. In the course of time Mirlinda expressed an interest in visiting Haydn in mid Wales, along with the other friend whom Haydn had met when asking for directions in Albania. He and Moira prayed about this. It was felt that the invitation should be given with one proviso. Mirlinda should also bring with then someone who could act as interpreter or translator for them.

It was arranged then for the April of 1998 that three Albanians should come into mid Wales for three weeks. This was the second time that Haydn had met Mirlinda and her friend, but the first time he met Etleva (Eva for short [pronounced Ever]). Eva's translation skills were excellent and was able to keep conversations flowing between the three Albanians and others around them.

They came to Heathrow and Haydn had to travel there from mid-Wales to collect them. It was Maundy Thursday in 1998 and he kept a lunchtime appointment with the churches together in Knighton and

District. He left, he thought, in plenty of time. But it had rained a lot and many of the main roads in Herefordshire were under water. This should have been his shortest and quickest route. Instead of picking up the M4 at Swindon he had to come back into Wales and pick up the M4 in Newport.

He arrived at the airport with just enough time to fill up with fuel, park the car, and get to the Arrivals gate.

He was there a few minutes when an announcement came over the sound system asking him to go to the information desk. He went there and a young immigration officer took him aside and asked if he was expecting anybody. He assured the officer that he was expecting three Albanians and produced their names.

Satisfied, the officer asked him where the three would be staying while in the UK; the three had the address in their luggage, but they were not allowed to access their luggage until they could produce a UK address. Haydn replied that they would be staying with him and his wife. He then gave his mid Wales address, and it rolled off his tongue as a natural speaker. Many others have problems with the Welsh place names.

The officer laughed pleasantly. 'No wonder they could not remember it', she said. With the formalities over, the officer went to where the Albanians were and Haydn went to the Arrivals gate.

Within five minutes they were through, and on the way back to mid-Wales. Straight down the M4 to Newport and then up through the Welsh countryside. The journey to the airport had been tiresome, but on the return journey the Albanians began to sing in Albanian: 'Let the weak say I am strong…'

This lifted Haydn's spirits. And before they knew it, they were home.

Haydn has stayed in touch with both Mirlinda and Eva. Mirlinda had some time in Turkey as a Christian worker before returning home to care for an elderly mother.

Mirlinda says, *'I am glad that I am a part of the story of your life as a believer... That's why I wrote in the comment... I am happy because you are the first person who spoke to me about the Lord Jesus as my Love and Saviour... That Evangelization was a blessing and hope for me...'*

While the three Albanians were in mid Wales, Haydn said to Moira that he thought Eva could and should spend some time in a bible college somewhere.

Eva had that gift way back then. Before Eva returned to Albania, he had a word with her and it was agreed that the various avenues be explored.

They left at the end of April 1998. Haydn gathered information of various UK colleges and made arrangements to go and see Eva. She had moved with her parents and brother to Greece. There was plenty of work in Greece for Albanians and the family went in search of work. Haydn went in the July of that year to stay with the family for five days.

The weather was hot – never below 30 – and Eva was working at two jobs. Each job was a full-time job in itself. By the end of the week, Eva's eyes were very sore from where she had been rubbing them for tiredness. It was suggested she went to a doctor, but she knew that if she went, she could lose one of her jobs. Eva alone could make that decision.

That was also true about the decision to go to Bible College. Haydn left all the information with Eva, who posed the question: 'Who would fund the course?' Haydn assured her that if it was right the money would be found.

As part of that process and application, Haydn could not act as a referee, for he had not known Eva for two years. But he and Moira were prepared to act as sponsor.

In the October of '98 Haydn was involved in a meeting at the college. The principal at the time saw Haydn in his office. There was a concern – and rightly so – about getting this right.

Haydn was asked how well he knew Eva. Haydn said that he and Moira were so convinced this was right that they would pay the first year's fees up front. They, with eyes of faith, could see that there was a diamond here which was worth pursuing.

Eva also prayed about the issue and by the September of 1999 she was a student at Cliff College. Eva came and studied at Cliff College, married Mick, has two lovely boys (twins) and trained for the Christian ministry in the Methodist church. Eva says, *'You are part of my story and I part of yours. And for that, I am thankful!'*

Haydn and Moira at the Wedding of Eva and Mick in England 2001

In Albania for the wedding blessing, which Haydn conducted

It was a joy and thrill for Haydn to help both Eva and Mirlinda on their way and they remain in his and Moira's prayers until the present time. He himself continued to grow in grace, faith, and love, as these relationships grew. They helped him grow closer to Christ.

In 2018, after Haydn had come back from Nepal, Moira and he had their usual holiday in Derbyshire. Some of the time was spent at the Festival at Cliff College. They also went walking.

One day they walked from Calver through Baslow, the grounds of Chatsworth, Endsor, and over Carlton Pastures to Bakewell. They had lunch together. While Moira spent time in Bakewell waiting for the bus back, Haydn decided he would walk back the way he came.

He had barely got onto Carlton pastures when his legs gave up. This was normally a busy area for walkers, but no one was around and there was no signal on his mobile. He could walk five steps and had to sit down for a few minutes. Having prayed hard at that point Haydn decided that to go forward was the better option than to go back.

He eventually got down into Chatsworth, caught a bus to Baslow. From there he phoned Moira who came in the car and picked him up. He eventually was able to see a doctor who told him that he had had a mini stroke.

In 2021, 2022, and 2023 Haydn had time in hospital.

The first two occasions were for his appendix: in '21 they were left in, but in'22 they had to come out. In '23 he had several falls because of his Parkinsons.

It took them a fortnight in hospital to sort it out and he was eventually sent home.

As he writes this section, he commits the future to God.

This week is Holy Week with Good Friday and Easter Sunday coming at the end of the week. Here is the reminder that Christ died upon that cross as the Lamb of God to take away our sins. Easter Sunday is the reminder that the Christ who died, was raised again from the dead. He has then conquered death because sin and the devil have been dealt with.

Those who know him reasonably well, know he loves his walking. It took his parents eighteen months to teach him to walk and talk, and another eighteen years telling him to sit down and be quiet!

Walking is his pastime. Five times he has attempted the Across Wales Charity Walk, a distance of, at least, 42 miles, on the Saturday nearest the longest day of the year.

The first of those attempts, Mountain Rescue met them all (200) at the first main checkpoint – 18 miles from the start – and took them off the walk. This was because of the heavy rain, and very low cloud hanging on Plynlimon. His fourth attempt, he arrived at the checkpoint at about 26 miles in, and he was unwell and could not finish. But attempts two, three, and five he managed to do the full distance in about 17 hours. He was asked if this was a flat walk and his response was: Across Wales - flat?

He has done the Pennine Way, the Peak Pilgrimage, the Glyndwr Way, the Yorkshire three peaks, and many other shorter walks. He had been attempting the Wales Coastal Path and have managed to do 550 of the 870 miles. But it looks as if this is one challenge too many.

It reminds us of the Christian life, which is described in the Bible as a walk with God. For us that walk might be short or long, but along a sunny beach, or in a rose garden, or by a river bank, or even a canal bank: for some it might even be urban streets; it is however a walk with the Saviour and is sweet to those who walk it.

For Haydn the walk with God has been long.

He called him early: 'Come, follow me!' And he followed, and is still following the most beloved Master. They have been on the mountain tops looking at grand 360 degrees views. The climbs up, and back down, have hurt the muscles in the legs, and made him short of breath, but it was well worth it for the grandeur of what he could see; but he could see it with his beloved Master, and be with Him.

Other times, he had been in landscape where the path was undefined, and underneath was peaty, boggy ground. In these places it would be easy either to fall into mire, or to lose a sense of direction. The bigger temptation then was simply to quit, to say, 'enough is enough'.

But the Master still says, 'Follow me!' So, he keeps following and He leads onwards and upwards.

Currently, he is in the valley, following the path of the river. The river is flowing the other way, that is downward so he is going upwards – slowly and gradually, but upwards. The walking, at the moment, is relatively easy, but who knows what might lie ahead.

Often children will ask, when on any kind of journey, 'Are we nearly there yet?' On this walk with his Lord and Saviour, he does not know the answer to that question. Yet each day at night time, he whispers quietly, 'A day's march nearer home.'

God is Faithful.

This is not

The End
Yet!